W9-CTJ-375

Ball-Handling Activities

by Janet A. Wessel and Ellen Curtis-Pierce

Fearon Teacher Aids
Belmont, California

Designed and Illustrated by Rose C. Sheifer

Copyright © 1990 by Fearon Teacher Aids,
500 Harbor Boulevard, Belmont, California 94002.
All rights reserved. No part of this book may be reproduced by any means, transmitted, or translated into a
machine language without written permission from the
publisher.

ISBN 0-8224-5351-7

Printed in the United States of America

1. 9 8 7 6 5 4 3 2 1

Contents

Contents

Meeting Special Needs of Children

AIMS OF THE PROGRAM

In any class, one or more students may be unable to play and perform basic motor skills effectively. If these students can't play, run, jump, and throw at an early age, they may be slow to develop essential motor skills as well as other basic learnings and social skills—or not develop them at all.

Play is a child's way of learning and integrating skills that will be used throughout life. Through play, children come to understand the world about them. Through play, children learn to move and move to learn. And as children gain play and motor skills, their feelings of self-worth and their positive self-images grow.

Most children learn to play and move through the activities of childhood. They learn by interacting with the environment and with their brothers and sisters and their peers. Handicapped children and other children with special needs often lack the opportunities to play with their peers. These children do not develop play and motor skills on their own. They need a structured, sequential curriculum to interact with their peers, gain feelings of self-worth, and achieve success—and the sooner these children can begin such a program, the better.

This Play and Motor Skills Activities Series presents a program of effective instruction strategies through which all children can achieve success in the general physical education program. It is not a pull-out program (that is, the child is not pulled out for therapy or special tutorial assistance); it is not a fix-it program (that is, the child is not segregated until all deficits are remediated). It is a positive program for each child to succeed in a play-and-motor-skills activity program. It is designed to help you, the teacher, set up sequential curricula, plan each child's instructional program, and teach effectively so that each child progresses toward desired learning outcomes.

Three Major Aims of the Program

1. To enable each child to perform basic play and motor skills at the level of his or her abilities;

2. To help each child use these skills in play and daily living activities to maximize his or her health, growth, and development, as well as joy in movement; and

3. To enhance each child's feelings of self-worth and self-confidence as a learner while moving to learn and learning to move.

BOOKS IN THE SERIES

There are eight books in this Play and Motor Skills Activities Series for preprimary through early primary grades, ages 3–7 years.

1. Locomotor Activities
2. Ball-Handling Activities
3. Stunts and Tumbling Activities
4. Health and Fitness Activities
5. Rhythmic Activities
6. Body Management Activities
7. Play Activities
8. Planning for Teaching

The seven activities books are designed to help teachers of children with handicaps and other special-needs children. Each book provides sequential curricula by skill levels. Each book is complete within its cover: sequential skills and teaching activities, games, action words, and checklists for the class's record of progress in each skill and an Individual Record of Progress (IRP) report.

Book 8, *Planning for Teaching*, is an essential companion to each of the seven activities books because it presents not only the steps for planning a teaching unit and providing for individual differences in each lesson, but it also includes a guide to incorporating social skills into units and lessons and also outlines a Home Activities Program. These two guides are particularly important for children with special needs. Because they often have limited opportunities to interact with their peers, these children need planned, sequential learning experiences to develop socially acceptable behaviors. And because special-needs children also often need extensive practice to retain a skill and generalize its use, a Home Activities Program, planned jointly by parents and teacher, can give them the necessary additional structured learning opportunities.

SEQUENTIAL CURRICULA: SUCCESS BY LEVELS

Each child and the teacher evaluate success. Success is built into the sequential curricula by levels of skills and teaching activities.

Each skill is divided into three levels: rudimentary Skill Level 1 and more refined Skill Levels 2 and 3. Each level is stated in observable behavioral movement terms. The skill levels become performance objectives. Children enter the sequential program at their own performance levels. As they add one small success to another and gain a new skill component or move to a higher skill level, they learn to listen, follow directions, practice, create, and play with others.

Within each skill level, your activities are sequenced, so the child can gain understanding progressively. Within each skill, you provide cues to meet each child's level of understanding and ability. The continuum of teaching cues is

1. verbal cues (action words) with physical assistance or prompts throughout the movement,

2. verbal cues and demonstrations,

3. verbal challenges and problem-solving cues such as "can you?" and

4. introduction of self-initiated learning activities.

GAMES

Game activities are identified for each performance objective by skill level in the seven activity books. At the end of each activity book is an alphabetized description of the games. This list includes the name of each game, formation, directions, equipment, skills involved in playing, and the type of play. Just before the list, you'll find selection criteria and ways to adapt games to different skill levels. Many of the game activities can be used to teach several objectives.

ACTION WORDS

Words for actions (step, look, catch, kick), objects (foot, ball, hand), and concepts (slow, fast, far) are used as verbal cues in teaching. These action words should be matched to the child's level of understanding. They provide a bridge to connect skill activities with other classroom learnings. In the seven activity books, action words are identified for each performance objective by skill level, and an alphabetized list of Action Words is provided at the beginning of each book. As you use this program, add words that are used in other classroom activities and delete those that the children are not ready to understand.

CHECKLISTS: A CHILD'S RECORD OF PROGRESS

In each activity book, you'll also find Individual and Class Records of Progress listing each performance objective. You can use one or both to record the entry performance level and progress of each child. The child's Individual Record of Progress can be used as part of the Individualized Educational Program (IEP). The teacher can record the child's entry performance level and progress on the child's IEP report form or use the end-of-the-year checklist report.

By observing each child performing the skills in class (e.g., during play, during teaching of the skill or in set-aside time), you can meet the special needs of each child. By using the checklists to record each child's entry level performance of objectives to be taught, you can develop an instructional plan for and evaluate the progress of each child.

Assign each child a learning task (skill component or skill level) based on lesson objectives, and plan lesson activities based on the entry performance level to help the child achieve success. Then use the checklists to record, evaluate, and report each child's progress to the parents. With this record of progress, you can review the teaching-learning activities and can make changes to improve them as necessary.

TEACHING STRATEGY

Direct Instruction

Direct Instruction is coaching on specific tasks at a skill level that allows each child to succeed. A structured and sequential curriculum of essential skills is the primary component of Direct Instruction. As the child progresses in learning, the teacher poses verbal challenges and problem-solving questions such as "can you?" and "show me!" Direct Instruction is based on the premise that success builds success and failure breeds failure.

Adaptive Instruction

Adaptive Instruction is modifying what is taught and how it is taught in order to respond to each child's special needs. Adaptive Instruction helps teachers become more responsive to individual needs. Teaching is based on the child's abilities, on what is to be taught in the lesson, and on what the child is to achieve at the end of instruction. Lesson plans are based on the child's entry performance level on the skills to be taught. Students are monitored during instruction, and the activities are adjusted to each student's needs. Positive reinforcement is provided and ways to correct the performance or behavior are immediately demonstrated.

Children enter the curriculum at different skill levels, and they learn at different rates. The sequential curriculum helps teachers to individualize the instruction for each child in the class. Thus, the same skill can be taught in a class that includes Betty, who enters at Skill Level 1, and James, who enters at Skill Level 3, because the activities are prescribed for the class or group, but the lesson is planned in order to focus on each child's learning task, and each child is working to achieve his or her own learning task. What is important is that each child master the essential skills at a level of performance that matches his or her abilities, interests, and joy.

Since children learn skills at different rates, you might want to use the following time estimates to allot instructional time for a child to make meaningful progress toward the desired level of performance. One or two skill components can usually be mastered in the instructional time available.

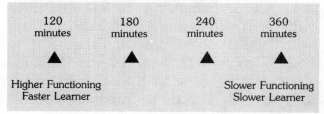

120 minutes	180 minutes	240 minutes	360 minutes
▲	▲	▲	▲

Higher Functioning Faster Learner   Slower Functioning Slower Learner

Ball-Handling Skills and Activities

INTRODUCTION

Goals for Each Child

1. To demonstrate the ability to perform basic ball-handling skills taught in the instructional program;

2. To use ball-handling skills in daily living activities in order to maximize healthy development and joy in movement; and

3. To gain greater feelings of self-worth and self-confidence and to gain greater ability in moving to learn and learning to move.

Ball-handling skills, including rolling, throwing, catching, bouncing, kicking, and hitting, are important fundamental skills for all children. The ability to handle and control a ball helps the child develop eye-hand and eye-foot coordination and the visual-tracking skills necessary for successful classroom learning.

Since early competence in ball-handling skills provides a basis for later games and sports activities, it is important that young children have an opportunity to develop these skills. Doing well in ball-handling games and sports strongly influences the child's self-image and successful participation with peers.

Children normally acquire ball-handling skills in an orderly, sequential manner during the preschool and early elementary years as they move from immature to refined, mature patterns. The development of ball-handling skills depends on the gradual maturing of both the motor and visual systems. But these systems do not develop at a consistent rate for any child. A child may experience a period of rapid change in motor behavior

with the acquisition of new skills followed by a plateau in which little change occurs. Or a child may acquire a skill but perform it inconsistently, because it takes time to integrate the skill into play and daily activities at home and at school.

The special-needs child, although following a similar sequential order, may proceed much more slowly and show greater inconsistency in the attainment of a given skill. Sometimes the skill may be absent from the child's repertoire due to lack of opportunity to participate in activities or to a condition that hinders acquisition of the skill.

Children with special needs in preschool through early elementary years require planned, structured, and sequenced motor and play activities to develop and maintain healthy growth equal to their potentials. This book presents three levels of activities for each ball-handling skill in the following order:

1. Rolling a ball   4. Bouncing a ball

2. Throwing a ball   5. Kicking a ball

3. Catching a ball   6. Hitting a ball

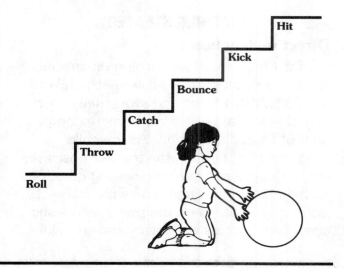

GETTING STARTED

To begin, decide which ball-handling skills you will teach. You can plan a unit or a week or a day or a year. You may decide to teach all skills in this book. Or you may select just a few. Review the checklist for each skill objective you select to teach. Become familiar with the skill components. Next, decide which action words and games you will use in teaching these skills.

Action Words

The words you use are teaching cues. Select ones your children will understand. For each of the ball-handling skills, action words are listed by skill level, and an alphabetized list of words for all the skills in this book is provided below. Circle the words you will use in teaching. If the words you selected prove too difficult for your students, cross them out. Add others that are more appropriate for your children. Star those words that work well.

ACTION	OBJECT	CONCEPT
Bend	Arm	Across
Bounce	Ball	Back
Catch	Balloon	Backward
Grasp	Beanbag	Behind
Hit	Blade	Between
Hold	Boxes	Both
Kick	Chair	Contact
Lift	Cones	Down
Move	Edge	Forward
Push	Eyes	Hard
Reach	Finger	Look
Release	Foot	Lower
Roll	Hand	More
Serve	Hockey stick	On
Sit	Hoops	One
Stand	Leg	Ready
Step	Line	Show me
Stop	Pail	Sideways
Swing	Push toy	Through
Throw	Sides	To
Walk	Stones	Toward
	Target	Under
	Toes	Up
	Wall	Upper
		Weight

Games and Play Activities

In each skill level, you'll find a list of games; select the activity matched to the skills you plan to teach. At the end of this book, you'll find a list of games along with a description of each of them. You'll note that some of the games can be used to teach more than one skill. Use this master list to note those games and play activities that work well and those that do not. Make your comments right on the game listed, or set up a similar format for the games you have selected and make your comments on that sheet. This kind of information can help you plan successful teaching activities.

Equipment

One or more of the following pieces of equipment will be needed for most of the ball-handling activities and games.

1. Whistle for signals
2. Balls (8" to 12" playground balls, whiffle balls, paper balls, balloons)
3. Targets
4. Traffic cones
5. Lines, colored tapes, or ropes taped to floor to mark the floor and to space equipment safely
6. Drum, tambourine
7. Various floor and ground surfaces (carpet, foam, sand, grass)
8. Beanbags and balls to throw into hoops, pails, boxes
9. Hockey sticks, broom handles

Space

Ball-handling activities require enough space for each child to move comfortably and safely. The size of the space depends on the equipment available for the activities and games selected and on the number of children in the class. A multipurpose room and a playground are desirable.

Health and Safety

Space and the equipment should be arranged for safety. Children with special visual needs may need a tour of the space and equipment before the lesson. A buddy can be assigned to be near the child when the lesson is taught. Children with special hearing needs may need to be close to the teacher or leader of the activity. The teacher should be positioned to observe all the children during the lesson activities.

Organization: Learning Centers

Learning centers are one of the best types of class organization. You can plan small group learning centers when you know each child's level of performance of the ball-handling skill to be taught. Learning centers can be used to group children by levels of ability or to mix children of different levels of ability. The number of learning centers and their purpose will depend on the number of teachers and support personnel: aides, parent volunteers, older peer models.

To set up a learning center, you should consider the following:

1. Purpose	Skills to be taught and practiced
2. Levels	Levels 1, 2, and 3, or only one, determined by size of class, space, equipment, support personnel
3. Grouping	Same or mixed skill levels
4. Physical setting	Location, such as playground or multipurpose room; equipment available; existing physical boundaries, such as walls, or space to make boundaries with chairs, benches, mats, tapes
5. Activities	Type of game or instructional activity, such as throwing, hitting, or kicking balls to or around targets or to others

LEARNING CENTERS: BALL-HANDLING ACTIVITIES

LEARNING CENTER 1

Location: Gymnasium

Skill: Throwing

Activity: Throwing balls at milk cartons, at targets, into hula hoop

Grouping: Children at same or different skill levels

LEARNING CENTER 2

Location: Playground

Skill: Hitting

Activity: Hitting balls at targets, around objects, under ropes

Grouping: Children at same or different skill levels

LEARNING CENTER 3

Location: Park

Skill: Kicking

Activity: Kicking up and down hills, around trash cans, to trees

Grouping: Children at same or different skill levels

Ball-Handling Activities

ROLLING A BALL: SKILL LEVEL 1

Performance Objective

The child with ability to sit can sit on the floor and roll (push) a 6- to 14-inch ball with one or both hands three consecutive times, demonstrating the following skill components:

Within a clear space of 10 feet, the child can

1. grasp ball with one or both hands and release in a forward direction and

2. roll or push the ball so that it travels an arm's length or more.

Action Words

Actions: Bend, grasp, hold, push, reach, roll, sit, stand

Objects: Ball, chair, hand(s), target, wall

Concepts: Across, behind, between, both, forward, hard, look, ready, show me, through, to

Games

- Ball in the Basket
- Ball Pass Relay
- Beach Ball Push
- Bowling Game
- Cage Ball Roll/Push
- Circle Strike Ball
- Hot Potato
- Obstacle Course
- Stride Ball
- Target Bowling

TEACHING ACTIVITIES

If a child requires assistance to respond,

1. give verbal cues and physical assistance.
Manipulate or guide the child through the entire skill. Sit behind the child, who has ball between legs. Hold the child by the wrists, and extend the elbows to push the ball. Give the child specific verbal instructions throughout (in sign language, bliss symbols, action cues), such as "Roll the ball, push hard."

2. give verbal cues with demonstration.
Use a model or have the child watch you roll the ball. Then have the child perform the action. Use specific verbal instructions (as in 1 above with the modeling). Say, "Roll the ball," "Put your hands on the ball," "Ready, set, go!"

If a child can respond without assistance,

3. give a verbal challenge in the form of a problem: "Who can . . . ?" "Show me how you can . . ."
a. Roll or push the ball to your friend (sitting at arm's distance away) from between your legs.
b. Roll or push the ball from either side of your legs.
c. Roll or push the ball to your friend back and forth, and keep moving farther away from your friend.
d. Variations: Tape handprints on the ball, and have child place his or her own hands on the handprints to roll or push the ball. Roll ball to music.

4. introduce self-initiated learning activities.
Set up the equipment and space for ball rolling. Provide time at the beginning of the lesson and free time for independent learning after the child understands the skills to be used. You may ask the child to create a game activity to play alone or with others (partner or small group), using the equipment.

5. Variations: Set up an obstacle course that includes foam shapes and other play equipment. Play a game, such as Ball in the Basket, Hot Potato, or Stride Ball, that incorporates rolling activities.

ROLLING A BALL: SKILL LEVEL 2

Performance Objective

The child with acquisition of Skill Level 1 can sit or stand and roll a 6- to 14-inch ball with one or both hands to a target 10 feet wide three consecutive times, demonstrating the following skill components:

Within a clear space of 10 feet, the child can

3. focus eyes on the target and
4. roll or push ball so that it travels 5 feet to a target, and then
5. roll or push ball so that it travels 10 feet to a target.

Skills to Review

1. Grasp ball with one or both hands and release in a forward direction and
2. roll or push ball so that it travels an arm's length or more.

Action Words

Actions: Bend, grasp, hold, push, reach, roll, sit, stand

Objects: Ball, chair, hand(s), target, wall

Concepts: Across, behind, between, both, forward, hard, look, ready, show me, through, to

Games

- Ball in the Basket
- Ball Pass Relay
- Beach Ball Push
- Bowling Game
- Cage Ball Roll/Push
- Circle Strike Ball
- Hot Potato
- Obstacle Course
- Stride Ball
- Target Bowling

TEACHING ACTIVITIES

If a child requires assistance to respond,

1. give verbal cues and physical assistance.
Manipulate or guide the child through the entire skill. Have the child learn to stand and roll or push a ball. Have the child straddle or stand and roll or push the ball a short distance. Give the child specific verbal instructions throughout (in sign language, bliss symbols, action cues), such as "Roll the ball," "Put your hands on the ball, push hard."

2. give verbal cues with demonstration.
Use a model or have the child watch you roll the ball. Then have the child stand and hold the ball and perform the action. Use specific verbal instructions (as in 1 above with the modeling). Say, "Roll the ball," "Put your hands on the ball," "Ready, set, go!"

If a child can respond without assistance,

3. give a verbal challenge in the form of a problem: "Who can . . . ?" "Show me how you can . . ."
a. Stand on the taped line and roll or push the ball down the line (vary lengths and colors).
b. Roll the ball to your partner.
c. Stand on a taped circle and roll the ball across the circle to a friend.
d. Roll the ball down a "track" (parallel boards, taped mats) to hit the target.

e. Roll the ball to the taped targets on the wall (vary target size and distance).

f. Roll the ball to the bowling pins (tin cans) and knock them down.

g. Variation: add music or drum; roll ball to music.

4. introduce self-initiated learning activities. Set up the equipment and space for rolling. Provide time at the beginning of the lesson and free time for independent learning after the child understands the skills to be used. You may ask the child to create a game activity to play alone or with others (partner or small group), using the equipment.

5. Variations: Set up an obstacle course that includes foam shapes and other play equipment. Play a game, such as Ball in the Basket, Hot Potato, or Stride Ball, that incorporates rolling activities.

ROLLING A BALL: SKILL LEVEL 3

Performance Objective

The child with acquisition of Skill Level 2 or a level of performance appropriate for the child's level of functioning can maintain that level over six weeks.

Given activities that require the skill, the child can

1. play two or more games listed below at home or school, and
2. play with equipment selected by teacher and parent(s).

Skills to Review

1. Level 1 rolling. Grasp ball with one or both hands and release in a forward direction and
2. roll or push ball so that it travels an arm's length or more.
3. Level 2 rolling. Focus eyes on the target and
4. roll or push ball so that it travels 5 feet to a target, and then
5. roll or push ball so that it travels 10 feet to a target.

Action Words

Actions: Bend, grasp, hold, push, reach, roll, sit, stand

Objects: Ball, chair, hand(s), target, wall

Concepts: Across, behind, between, both, forward, hard, look, ready, show me, through, to

Games

- Ball in the Basket
- Ball Pass Relay
- Beach Ball Push
- Bowling Game
- Cage Ball Roll/Push
- Circle Strike Ball
- Hot Potato
- Obstacle Course
- Stride Ball
- Target Bowling

TEACHING ACTIVITIES FOR MAINTENANCE

In Teaching

1. Provide the child with teaching cues (verbal and nonverbal, such as demonstration, modeling, imitating) for rolling a ball that involve the skill components the child has achieved in compatible teaching and play activities. Bring to the child's attention the skill components he or she has already achieved. Provide positive reinforcement and feedback for the child.

2. Use games that require rolling a ball and that involve imitating, modeling, and demonstrating.

3. Observe and assess each child's maintenance at the end of two weeks. Repeat at the end of four weeks (if maintained) and six weeks after initial date of attainment.

▲ Box in the skill level to be maintained on the child's Class Record of Progress. Note the date the child attained target level of performance (defined by teacher alone or co-planned with parents).

▲ Two weeks after attainment, observe the child. Is the level maintained? If child does not demonstrate the skill components at the desired level of performance, indicate the skill components that need reteaching or reinforcing in the comments sheet on the Class Record of Progress. Reschedule teaching time, and co-plan with parents the home activities necessary to reinforce child's achievement of the skill components and maintenance of attainment.

▲ Continue to observe the child, and reteach and reinforce until the child maintains that level of performance for six weeks.

▲ Plan teaching activities incorporating these components so that the child can continually use and reinforce them and can acquire new ones over the year.

▲ When the child can understand it, make a checklist poster illustrating the child's achievements. Bring the child's attention to these skill components in various compatible play and game activities throughout the year. Have the child help others—a partner or a small group.

In Co-Planning with Parent(s)

1. Encourage the parent(s) to reinforce the child's achievement of the skill components in everyday play and living activities in the home.

▲ Provide key action words for the parent(s) to emphasize.

▲ Give the parent(s) a list of play and games to use in playing with the child, thus reinforcing the skill components the child has achieved and needs support to maintain.

▲ Give the parent(s) a list of ball-handling activities that can be done at home with the child, such as

   a. Rolling the ball down the tape marks and hitting the rectangle target.

   b. Rolling the ball around the room and hitting the geometric shapes on the floor.

   c. Rolling the ball through the hoops.

   d. Rolling the ball to objects that make noise (such as wind chimes).

   e. Rolling the ball between the legs of chairs, down an incline, on a bench.

   f. Rolling the ball and knocking the bowling pins down from 8 feet away.

   g. Variation: Add music or a drum and roll ball to music.

2. Set up a time every two weeks to interact with the parent(s) and exchange feedback on the child's progress.

THROWING A BALL: SKILL LEVEL 1

Performance Objective

The child with ability to grasp and release a ball in a forward direction can release a 2- to 3-inch ball in a forward direction three consecutive times, demonstrating the following skill components:

Within a clear space of 20 feet, the child can

1. while grasping ball with one hand, release ball in forward direction with
2. arm extended forward as ball is released;
3. ball travels forward 5 feet in air.

Action Words

Actions: Hold, release, throw

Objects: Arm, ball, eyes, hand, line, stones, target

Concepts: Back, down, forward, look, ready, show me, to, up, weight

Games

- Ball in the Basket
- Bowling Game
- Call Ball
- Cleaning Out the Backyard
- Hot Potato
- Leader, Class
- Net Ball
- Obstacle Course
- Paper Ball Play
- Shotgun
- Stride Ball
- Target Practice
- Toss-Jump-Pick

TEACHING ACTIVITIES

If a child requires assistance to respond,

1. give verbal cues and physical assistance.
Manipulate or guide the child through the entire skill. Manipulate the child into an arm-extended position to show how to toss the ball. Give the child specific verbal instructions throughout (in sign language, bliss symbols, action cues), such as "Throw the ball," "Ready, set, go!"

2. give verbal cues with demonstration.
Use a model or have the child watch you throw a ball. The child should sit where he or she can see both you and a target. Pick up the ball, and throw it at the target. Then have the child perform the action. Use specific verbal instructions (as in 1 above with the modeling). Say, "Throw the ball," "Put your hands on the ball," "Ready, set, go!"

If a child can respond without assistance,

3. give a verbal challenge in the form of a problem: "Who can . . . ?" "Show me how you can . . ."
a. Toss the whiffle ball attached to the string forward.
b. Toss the ball to me (from 3 feet away).
c. Toss the ball against the wall, retrieve it, and toss it again.
d. Toss the ball back and forth to a partner.
e. Variation: Toss the ball to music.

4. introduce self-initiated learning activities.
Set up the equipment and space for throwing. Provide time at the beginning of the lesson and free time for independent learning after the child understands the skills to be used. You may ask the child to create a game activity to play alone or with others (partner or small group), using the equipment.

5. Variations: Set up an obstacle course that includes foam shapes and other play equipment. Play a game, such as Ball in the Basket or Hot Potato, that incorporates throwing activities.

THROWING A BALL: SKILL LEVEL 2

Performance Objective

The child with acquisition of Skill Level 1 can throw a 2- to 3-inch ball toward a target three consecutive times, demonstrating the following skill components:

Within a clear space of 20 feet, the child can

4. focus eyes on target,
5. draw back arm in preparation to throw, and
6. shift weight to nonthrowing side as ball is released;
7. ball travels 10 feet in air toward target.

Skills to Review

1. While grasping ball with one hand, release ball in forward direction with
2. arm extended forward as ball is released;
3. ball travels forward 5 feet in air.

Action Words

Actions: Hold, release, throw

Objects: Arm, ball, eyes, hand, line, stones, target

Concepts: Back, down, forward, look, ready, show me, to, up, weight

Games

- Ball in the Basket
- Bowling Game
- Call Ball
- Cleaning out the Backyard
- Hot Potato
- Leader, Class
- Net Ball
- Obstacle Course
- Paper Ball Play
- Shotgun
- Stride Ball
- Target Practice
- Toss-Jump-Pick

TEACHING ACTIVITIES

If a child requires assistance to respond,

1. give verbal cues and physical assistance.
Manipulate or guide the child through the entire skill. Manipulate the child into an arm-extended position to show how to toss the ball. Give the child specific verbal instructions throughout (in sign language, bliss symbols, action cues), such as "Throw the ball," "Ready, set, go!"

2. give verbal cues with demonstration.
Use a model or have the child watch you throw a ball. The child should sit where he or she can see both you and a target. Pick up the ball and throw it at the target. Then have the child perform the action. Use specific verbal instructions (as in 1 above with the modeling). Say, "Throw the ball," "Put your hands on the ball," "Ready, set, go!"

If a child can respond without assistance,

3. give a verbal challenge in the form of a problem: "Who can . . . ?" "Show me how you can . . ."
a. Throw the ball at the merry-go-round as it moves around.
b. Throw the beanbag at the wagons on the playground.

c. Toss the ball at the milk cartons sitting on the backyard fence.

d. Toss the ball in the throwing games, such as Net Ball, Toss-Jump-Pick, or Leader, Class.

e. Toss the ball on the top of the hill. Run up and retrieve it.

f. Throw snowballs at trees or buckets.

g. Throw wet sponges at the wall and make designs.

h. Pick up the trash and throw it away.

4. introduce self-initiated learning activities. Set up the equipment and space for throwing. Provide time at the beginning of the lesson and free time for independent learning after the child understands the skills to be used. You may ask the child to create a game activity to play alone or with others (partner or small group), using the equipment.

5. Variations: Set up an obstacle course that includes foam shapes and other play equipment. Play a game, such as Ball in the Basket or Hot Potato, that incorporates throwing activities.

THROWING A BALL: SKILL LEVEL 3

Performance Objective

The child with acquisition of Skill Level 2 or a level of performance appropriate for the child's level of functioning can maintain that level over six weeks.

Given activities that require the skill, the child can

1. play two or more games listed below at home or school, and
2. play with equipment selected by teacher and parent(s).

Skills to Review

1. Level 1 throwing. While grasping ball with one hand, release ball in forward direction with
2. arm extended forward as ball is released;
3. ball travels forward 5 feet in air.
4. Level 2 throwing. Focus eyes on the target,
5. draw back arm in preparation to throw, and
6. shift weight to nonthrowing side as ball is released;
7. ball travels 10 feet in air toward target.

Action Words

Actions: Hold, release, throw

Objects: Arm, ball, eyes, hand, line, stones, target

Concepts: Back, down, forward, look, ready, show me, to, up, weight

Games

- Ball in the Basket
- Bowling Game
- Call Ball
- Cleaning out the Backyard
- Hot Potato
- Leader, Class
- Net Ball
- Obstacle Course
- Paper Ball Play
- Shotgun
- Stride Ball
- Target Practice
- Toss-Jump-Pick

TEACHING ACTIVITIES FOR MAINTENANCE

In Teaching

1. Provide the child with teaching cues (verbal and nonverbal, such as demonstration, modeling, imitating) for throwing a ball that involve the skill components the child has achieved in compatible teaching and play activities. Bring to the child's attention the skill components he or she has already achieved. Provide positive reinforcement and feedback for the child.
2. Use games that require throwing a ball and that involve imitating, modeling, and demonstrating.
3. Observe and assess each child's maintenance at the end of two weeks. Repeat at the end of four weeks (if maintained) and six weeks after initial date of attainment.

▲ Box in the skill level to be maintained on the child's Class Record of Progress. Note the date the child attained target level of performance (defined by teacher alone or co-planned with parents).

▲ Two weeks after attainment, observe the child. Is the level maintained? If child does not demonstrate the skill components at the desired level of performance, indicate the skill components that need reteaching or reinforcing in the comments sheet on the Class Record of Progress. Reschedule teaching time, and co-plan with parents the home activities necessary to reinforce child's achievement of the skill components and maintenance of attainment.

▲ Continue to observe the child, and reteach and reinforce until the child maintains that level of performance for six weeks.

▲ Plan teaching activities incorporating these components so that the child can continually use and reinforce them and can acquire new ones over the year.

▲ When the child can understand it, make a check-list poster illustrating the child's achievements. Bring the child's attention to these skill components in various compatible play and game activities throughout the year. Have the child help others—a partner or a small group.

In Co-Planning with Parent(s)

1. Encourage the parent(s) to reinforce the child's achievement of the skill components in everyday play and living activities in the home.

▲ Provide key action words for the parent(s) to emphasize.

▲ Give the parent(s) a list of play and games to use in playing with the child, thus reinforcing the skill components the child has achieved and needs support to maintain.

▲ Give the parent(s) a list of throwing activities that can be done at home with the child, such as
   a. Throwing the ball at the merry-go-round as it moves around.
   b. Throwing the beanbag at the wagons on the playground.
   c. Tossing the ball at the milk cartons sitting on the backyard fence.
   d. Tossing the ball in the throwing games such as Net Ball, and Toss-Jump-Pick, or Leader, Class.
   e. Tossing the ball on the top of the hill and running up and retrieving it.
   f. Throwing snowballs at trees or buckets.
   g. Throwing wet sponges at the wall and making designs.
   h. Picking up the trash and throwing it away.

2. Set up a time every two weeks to interact with the parent(s) and exchange feedback on the child's progress.

CATCHING A BALL: SKILL LEVEL 1

Performance Objective

The child with ability to sit on the floor and grasp a ball can trap or catch a 6- to 14-inch ball rolled slowly (2 to 4 feet per second) and directly to the child from a distance of 3 feet three consecutive times, demonstrating the following skill components:

Within a clear space of 15 feet, the child can
1. focus eyes on ball and
2. stop ball with hands or hands and arms.

Action Words

Actions: Bend, bounce, catch, hold, reach, roll, sit, stop

Objects: Arm, ball, balloon, hands, push toy, sides, toes

Concepts: Down, look, on, ready, show me, toward, up

Games

- Ball in the Basket
- Boundary Ball
- Call Ball
- Catching Balloons and Soap Bubbles
- Hot Potato
- Monkey in the Middle
- Scoop Catch
- Stride Ball
- Throw, Rebound, Catch

TEACHING ACTIVITIES

If a child requires assistance to respond,

1. give verbal cues and physical assistance.
Manipulate or guide the child through the entire skill. Sit behind or beside the child and have aide roll ball to the child. Physically prompt child by positioning his or her hands to catch rolled ball. Give the child specific verbal instructions throughout (in sign language, bliss symbols, action cues), such as "Catch the ball," "Look at the ball roll," "Catch it," "Hold it."

2. give verbal cues with demonstration.
Use a model or have the child watch you sit and have aide roll ball to you. You catch the ball. Then have the child perform the action. Use specific verbal instructions (as in 1 above with the modeling).

If a child can respond without assistance,

3. give a verbal challenge in the form of a problem: "Who can . . . ?" "Show me how you can . . ."
a. Trap or catch rolling balls from your partner and vice versa. Keep increasing and decreasing the distances.
b. Roll ball to wall and trap or catch the ball when it rolls back.
c. Catch nerf ball or a balloon.

4. introduce self-initiated learning activities.
Set up the equipment and space for catching skills. Provide time at the beginning of the lesson and free time for independent learning after the child understands the skills to be used. You may ask the child to create a game activity to play alone or with others (partner or small group), using the equipment.

5. Variations: Set up an obstacle course that includes foam shapes and other play equipment. Play a game, such as Ball in the Basket, Hot Potato, Name Ball, or Monkey in the Middle, that incorporates catching activities.

CATICHING A BALL: SKILL LEVEL 2

Performance Objective

The child with acquisition of Skill Level 1, while sitting or standing on a chair, can trap or catch a 6- to 14-inch ball bounced or dropped on the floor to a height between the child's waist and shoulders and no more than 18 inches in front of the child's body three consecutive times, demonstrating the following skill components:

Within a clear space of 15 feet, the child can

3. focus eyes on ball,
4. extend arms in preparation to catch ball, with elbows at sides,
5. contact and control ball with hands or hands and arms after one bounce, and
6. bend elbows to absorb force of ball.

Skills to Review

1. Focus eyes on ball and
2. stop ball with hands or hands and arms.

Action Words

Actions: Bend, bounce, catch, hold, reach, roll, sit, stop

Objects: Arm, ball, balloon, hands, push toy, sides, toes

Concepts: Down, look, on, ready, show me, toward, up

Games

- Ball in the Basket
- Boundary Ball
- Call Ball
- Catching Balloons and Soap Bubbles
- Hot Potato
- Monkey in the Middle
- Scoop Catch
- Stride Ball
- Throw, Rebound, Catch

TEACHING ACTIVITIES

If a child requires assistance to respond,

1. give verbal cues and physical assistance.
Manipulate or guide the child through the entire skill. Sit behind or beside the child, and grasp his or her hands, assisting the child to catch the ball with hands, elbows flexed. Give the child specific verbal instructions throughout (in sign language, bliss symbols, action cues), such as "Get ready to catch the ball," "Hold your hands out," "Catch the ball," "Trap the ball."

2. give verbal cues with demonstration.
Use a model or have the child watch you stand in preparatory position with hands in front of body, elbows flexed. Have an aide throw you a ball. Reach with your hands to catch the ball, extending the arms for ball contact. Use verbal cues throughout, "Watch me catch the ball. My hands reach out for the ball. Now you catch the ball," "Reach," "Catch," "Hold, trap."

If a child can respond without assistance,

3. give a verbal challenge in the form of a problem: "Who can . . . ?" "Show me how you can . . ."

a. Catch the brightly colored beach ball.

b. Catch a ball thrown from your partner.

c. Roll the ball and run to catch it.

d. Throw it high, turn around, clap your hands, and catch it.

e. Variations: Catch to the beat of the drum. Use different types of objects to catch (nerf ball, beanbag, balloons, whiffle ball).

4. introduce self-initiated learning activities. Set up the equipment and space for catching skills. Provide time at the beginning of the lesson and free time for independent learning after the child understands the skills to be used. You may ask the child to create a game activity to play alone or with others (partner or small group), using the equipment.

5. Variations: Set up an obstacle course that includes foam shapes and other play equipment. Play a game, such as Ball in the Basket, Hot Potato, Name Ball, or Monkey in the Middle, that incorporates catching a ball.

CATCHING A BALL: SKILL LEVEL 3

Performance Objective

The child with acquisition of Skill Level 2 or a level of performance appropriate for the child's level of functioning can maintain that level over six weeks.

Given activities that require the skill, the child can
1. play two or more games listed below at home or school, and
2. play with equipment selected by teacher and parent(s).

Skills to Review

1. Level 1 catching. Focus eyes on ball and
2. stop ball with hands or hands and arms.
3. Level 2 catching. Focus eyes on ball,
4. extend arms in preparation to catch ball, with elbows at sides,
5. contact and control ball with hands or hands and arms after one bounce, and
6. bend elbows to absorb force of ball.

Action Words

Actions: Bend, bounce, catch, hold, reach, roll, sit, stop

Objects: Arm, ball, balloon, hands, push toy, sides, toes

Concepts: Down, look, on, ready, show me, toward, up

Games

- Ball in the Basket
- Boundary Ball
- Call Ball
- Catching Balloons and Soap Bubbles
- Hot Potato
- Monkey in the Middle
- Scoop Catch
- Stride Ball
- Throw, Rebound, Catch

TEACHING ACTIVITIES FOR MAINTENANCE

In Teaching

1. Provide the child with teaching cues (verbal and nonverbal, such as demonstration, modeling, imitating) for catching a ball that involve the skill components the child has achieved in compatible teaching and play activities. Bring to the child's attention the skill components he or she has already achieved. Provide positive reinforcement and feedback for the child.

2. Use games that require catching a ball and that involve imitating, modeling, and demonstrating.

3. Observe and assess each child's maintenance at the end of two weeks. Repeat at the end of four weeks (if maintained) and six weeks after initial date of attainment.

▲ Box in the skill level to be maintained on the child's Class Record of Progress. Note the date the child attained target level of performance (defined by teacher alone or co-planned with parents).

▲ Two weeks after attainment, observe the child. Is the level maintained? If child does not demonstrate the skill components at the desired level of performance, indicate the skill components that need reteaching or reinforcing in the comments sheet on the Class Record of Progress. Reschedule teaching time, and co-plan with parents the home activities necessary to reinforce child's achievement of the skill components and maintenance of attainment.

▲ Continue to observe the child, and reteach and reinforce until the child maintains that level of performance for six weeks.

▲ Plan teaching activities incorporating these components so that the child can continually use and reinforce them and can acquire new ones over the year.

▲ When the child can understand it, make a checklist poster illustrating the child's achievements. Bring the child's attention to these skill components in various compatible play and game activities throughout the year. Have the child help others—a partner or a small group.

In Co-Planning with Parent(s)

1. Encourage the parent(s) to reinforce the child's achievement of the skill components in everyday play and living activities in the home.

▲ Provide key action words for the parent(s) to emphasize.

▲ Give the parent(s) a list of play and games to use in playing with the child, thus reinforcing the skill components the child has achieved and needs support to maintain.

▲ Give the parent(s) a list of catching activities that can be done at home with the child, such as
   a. Catching a ball thrown over a net.
   b. Catching a ball thrown in the circle game, Monkey in the Middle.
   c. Catching a ball thrown over the backyard fence.
   d. Catching a ball thrown across the sidewalk or driveway.
   e. Throwing a ball in the air and running to catch it before it bounces.
   f. Variation: Catch a variety of objects (nerf ball, whiffle ball, tennis ball, volleyball).

2. Set up a time every two weeks to interact with the parent(s) and exchange feedback on the child's progress.

BOUNCING A BALL: SKILL LEVEL 1

Performance Objective

The child with ability to hit a ball can hit the ball (held by the teacher) downward with one or both hands three consecutive times, demonstrating the following skill components:

Within a clear space of 15 feet, the child can

1. focus eyes on ball and
2. hit or push the ball downward with one or both hands three times.

Action Words

Actions: Hit, kick, move, push, step, stop, swing, walk

Objects: Ball, cones, hands

Concepts: Backward, both, forward, look, one, ready, show me, sideways

Games

- Bounce Ball Relay
- Boundary Ball
- Call Ball
- Circle Strike Ball
- Hot Potato
- Net Ball
- Obstacle Course
- Shotgun
- Stride Ball

TEACHING ACTIVITIES

If a child requires assistance to respond,

1. give verbal cues and physical assistance.
Manipulate or guide the child through the entire skill. Have an aide or another student hold the ball with two hands next to the child. Place the child's hands on each side of the ball, and put your hands over the child's hands. Open the child's hands to release the ball. Give the child specific verbal instructions throughout (in sign language, bliss symbols, action cues), such as "Bounce the ball," "Drop it, then hit it," "Ready, go!"

2. give verbal cues with demonstration.
Use a model or have the child watch you demonstrate the skill. While the child watches, have an aide or another child hold the ball. You hit the ball downward out of aide's hands. Then have the child perform the action. Use specific verbal instructions (as in 1 above with the modeling).

If a child can respond without assistance,

3. give a verbal challenge in the form of a problem: "Who can . . . ?" "Show me how you can . . ."
a. Hit the ball downward out of my hands.
b. Hit the ball downward out of your partner's hands and vice versa.
c. Hit these balls (of different sizes), one at a time, downward after they rebound.
d. Variation: Use handprints on ball or tape mark to show hand placement. Then hit ball on various surfaces (hard floor, carpet, cement).

4. introduce self-initiated learning activities.
Set up the equipment and space for bouncing skills. Provide time at the beginning of the lesson and free time for independent learning after the child understands the skills to be used. You may ask the child to create a game activity to play alone or with others (partner or small group), using the equipment.

5. Variations: Set up an obstacle course that includes foam shapes and other play equipment. Play a game, such as Hot Potato, Freeze, or Call Ball, that incorporates bouncing a ball.

Performance Objective

The child with acquisition of Skill Level 1 can bounce an 8- to 12-inch ball with one or both hands three consecutive times, demonstrating the following skill components:

Within a clear space of 15 feet, the child can

3. drop ball and hit or push it downward with one or both hands one time as it bounces, with *eyes* focused on ball, and then

4. hit or push ball downward three or more times as it bounces, with *eyes* focused on the ball.

 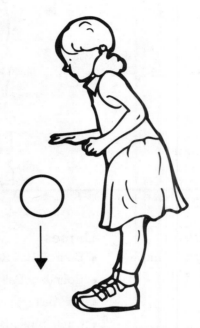

Skills to Review

1. Focus eyes on ball and
2. hit or push ball downward with one or both hands three times.

Action Words

Actions: Hit, kick, move, push, step, stop, swing, walk

Objects: Ball, cones, hands

Concepts: Backward, both, forward, look, one, ready, show me, sideways

Games

- Bounce Ball Relay
- Boundary Ball
- Call Ball
- Circle Strike Ball
- Hot Potato
- Net Ball
- Obstacle Course
- Shotgun
- Stride Ball

TEACHING ACTIVITIES

If a child requires assistance to respond,

1. give verbal cues and physical assistance.
Manipulate or guide the child through the *entire* skill. Have an aide or another student hold the ball with two hands next to the child. Place the child's hands on each side of the ball, and put your hands over the child's hands. Open the child's hands to release the ball. Give the child specific verbal instructions throughout (in sign language, bliss symbols, action cues), such as "Bounce the ball," "Drop it, then hit it," "Ready, go!"

2. give verbal cues with demonstration.
Use a model or have the child watch you demonstrate the skill. Drop the ball, and push it downward with your wrist; as it rebounds push it down again. Then have the child perform the action. Use specific verbal instructions (as in 1 above with the modeling).

If a child can respond without assistance,

3. give a verbal challenge in the form of a problem: "Who can . . . ?" "Show me how you can . . ."

a. Bounce the ball with one hand, then two hands.

b. Bounce the large ball three times, then bounce the small ball.

c. Bounce the ball around the cones scattered around the room, but don't hit the cones.

d. Bounce the ball on the taped square on the floor. How many times can you bounce it?

e. Variation: Bounce ball to music.

4. introduce self-initiated learning activities.
Set up the equipment and space for bouncing skills. Provide time at the beginning of the lesson and free time for independent learning after the child understands the skills to be used. You may ask the child to create a game activity to play alone or with others (partner or small group), using the equipment.

5. Variations: Set up an obstacle course that includes foam shapes and other play equipment. Play a game, such as Hot Potato, Freeze, or Call Ball, that incorporates bouncing a ball.

BOUNCING A BALL: SKILL LEVEL 3

Performance Objective

The child with acquisition of Skill Level 2 or a level of performance appropriate for the child's level of functioning can maintain that level over six weeks.

Given activities that require the skill, the child can

1. play two or more games listed below at home or school, and
2. play with equipment selected by teacher and parent(s).

Skills to Review

1. Level 1 bouncing. Focus eyes on ball and
2. hit or push ball downward with one or both hands three times.
3. Level 2 bouncing. Drop ball and hit or push it three or more times, with eyes focused on ball, and then
4. hit or push ball downward three or more times as it bounces, with eyes focused on ball.

Action Words

Actions: Hit, kick, move, push, step, stop, swing, walk

Objects: Ball, cones, hands

Concepts: Backward, both, forward, look, one, ready, show me, sideways

Games

- Bounce Ball Relay
- Boundary Ball
- Call Ball
- Circle Strike Ball
- Hot Potato
- Net Ball
- Obstacle Course
- Shotgun
- Stride Ball

TEACHING ACTIVITIES FOR MAINTENANCE

In Teaching

1. Provide the child with teaching cues (verbal and nonverbal, such as demonstration, modeling, imitating) for bouncing a ball that involve the skill components the child has achieved in compatible teaching and play activities. Bring to the child's attention the skill components he or she has already achieved. Provide positive reinforcement and feedback for the child.

2. Use games that require bouncing a ball and that involve imitating, modeling, and demonstrating.

3. Observe and assess each child's maintenance at the end of two weeks. Repeat at the end of four weeks (if maintained) and six weeks after initial date of attainment.

▲ Box in the skill level to be maintained on the child's Class Record of Progress. Note the date the child attained target level of performance (defined by teacher alone or co-planned with parents).

▲ Two weeks after attainment, observe the child. Is the level maintained? If child does not demonstrate the skill components at the desired level of performance, indicate the skill components that need reteaching or reinforcing in the comments sheet on the Class Record of Progress. Reschedule teaching time, and co-plan with parents the home activities necessary to reinforce child's achievement of the skill components and maintenance of attainment.

▲ Continue to observe the child, and reteach and reinforce until the child maintains that level of performance for six weeks.

▲ Plan teaching activities incorporating these components so that the child can continually use and reinforce them and can acquire new ones over the year.

▲ When the child can understand it, make a checklist poster illustrating the child's achievements. Bring the child's attention to these skill components in various compatible play and game activities throughout the year. Have the child help others—a partner or a small group.

In Co-Planning with Parent(s)

1. Encourage the parent(s) to reinforce the child's achievement of the skill components in everyday play and living activities in the home.

▲ Provide key action words for the parent(s) to emphasize.

▲ Give the parent(s) a list of play and games to use in playing with the child, thus reinforcing the skill components the child has achieved and needs support to maintain.

▲ Give the parent(s) a list of ball-bouncing activities that can be done at home with the child, such as
   a. Bouncing the ball with one hand, then two hands.
   b. Bouncing the large ball three times, then bouncing the small ball.
   c. Bouncing the ball around the cones scattered around the room, but not hitting the cones.
   d. Bouncing the ball on the taped square on the floor. How many times can you bounce it?
   e. Variation: Bounce the ball to music.

2. Set up a time every two weeks to interact with the parent(s) and exchange feedback on the child's progress.

Performance Objective

The child with ability to sit or stand and kick a stationary ball can kick a stationary 8- to 12-inch ball three consecutive times, demonstrating the following skill components:

Within a clear space of 15 feet, the child can

1. focus eyes on ball and,
2. swinging lower leg forward, contact ball with foot and
3. kick the ball so that it travels forward 8 feet.

Action Words

Actions: Kick, move, step, stop, swing, walk

Objects: Ball, boxes, cones, foot, leg

Concepts: Backward, contact, forward, look, lower, ready, show me, sideways

Games

- Ball in the Basket
- Bowling Game
- Call Ball
- Circle Strike Ball
- Hot Potato
- Keep It Up
- Kick the Can
- Kick to the Target
- Modifed Soccer
- Obstacle Course
- Scooter Kickball
- Stride Ball

TEACHING ACTIVITIES

If a child requires assistance to respond,

1. give verbal cues and physical assistance. Manipulate or guide the child through the entire skill. Stand behind the child, holding on to one of the child's hands for support. Have the child step forward on nonkicking foot, and then push lower leg of kicking foot backward in preparation to kick. Kick the ball forward. Give the child specific verbal instructions throughout (in sign language, bliss symbols, action cues), such as "Look at the ball," "Let's kick it," "Here it comes."

2. give verbal cues with demonstration.

Use a model or have the child watch you stand and kick the ball. Step forward with nonkicking foot, swing lower leg backward in preparation for kick, then kick the ball so that it travels forward at least six feet. Then have the child perform the action. Use specific verbal instructions (as in 1 above with the modeling).

If a child can respond without assistance,

3. give a verbal challenge in the form of a problem: "Who can . . . ?" "Show me how you can . . ."

a. Kick the ball being rolled to you. Run to first base and back to home.

b. Kick the ball at the wall and keep moving to kick it again and again.

c. Have your partner roll you a ball to kick; then you do the same.

d. Kick the rolled ball between two cones.

e. Kick the ball and then run after it.

f. Variation: Kick rolled ball to music.

4. introduce self-initiated learning activities. Set up the equipment and space for kicking skills. Provide time at the beginning of the lesson and free time for independent learning after the child understands the skills to be used. You may ask the child to create a game activity to play alone or with others (partner or small group), using the equipment.

5. Variations: Set up an obstacle course that includes foam shapes and other play equipment. Play a game, such as Ball in the Basket, Hot Potato, Keep It Up, Kick the Can, or Kick the Target, that incorporates kicking a ball.

KICKING A BALL: SKILL LEVEL 2

Performance Objective

The child with acquisition of Skill Level 1 can kick an 8- to 12-inch ball that is rolled to the child from 5 feet away three consecutive times, demonstrating the following skill components:

Within a clear space of 15 feet, the child can

4. step forward with nonkicking leg, eyes focused on rolling ball and
5. swing lower leg backward in preparation to kick, and then
6. swing leg forward, contact ball with foot, and kick ball so that it travels forward 8 feet.

Skills to Review

1. Focus eyes on ball and,
2. swinging lower leg forward, contact ball with foot and
3. kick ball so that it travels forward 8 feet.

Action Words

Actions: Kick, move, step, stop, swing, walk

Objects: Ball, boxes, cones, foot, leg

Concepts: Backward, contact, forward, look, lower, ready, show me, sideways

Games

- Ball in the Basket
- Bowling Game
- Call Ball
- Circle Strike Ball
- Hot Potato
- Keep It Up
- Kick the Can
- Kick to the Target
- Modified Soccer
- Obstacle Course
- Scooter Kickball
- Stride Ball

TEACHING ACTIVITIES

If a child requires assistance to respond,

1. give verbal cues and physical assistance.
Manipulate or guide the child through the entire skill. Stand behind the child, holding on to one of the child's hands for support. Have the child step forward on nonkicking foot, and then push lower leg of kicking foot backward in preparation to kick. Kick the ball forward. Give the child specific verbal instructions throughout (in sign language, bliss symbols, action cues), such as "Look at the ball," "Let's kick it," "Here it comes."

2. give verbal cues with demonstration.
Use a model or have the child watch you stand and kick the ball. Step forward with nonkicking foot, swing lower leg backward in preparation for kick, then kick the ball so that it travels forward at least 6 feet. Then have the child perform the action. Use specific verbal instructions (as in 1 above with the modeling).

If a child can respond without assistance,

3. give a verbal challenge in the form of a problem: "Who can . . . ?" "Show me how you can . . ."

a. Kick the ball at the wall and kick it again.

b. Walk around the circle and kick each ball that you come to.

c. Kick the ball back and forth to your partner.

d. Kick the ball into the cardboard boxes around the room.

e. Take a step over the rope and then kick the ball as far as you can.

f. Kick the ball at the clown target. Can you kick it into the clown's mouth?

g. Variation: Kick to music.

4. introduce self-initiated learning activities. Set up the equipment and space for kicking skills. Provide time at the beginning of the lesson and free time for independent learning after the child understands the skills to be used. You may ask the child to create a game activity to play alone or with others (partner or small group), using the equipment.

5. Variations: Set up an obstacle course that includes foam shapes and other play equipment. Play a game, such as Ball in the Basket, Hot Potato, Keep It Up, Kick the Can, or Kick the Target, that incorporates kicking a ball.

KICKING A BALL: SKILL LEVEL 3

Performance Objective

The child with acquisition of Skill Level 2 or a level of performance appropriate for the child's level of functioning can maintain that level over six weeks.

Given activities that require the skill, the child can

1. play two or more games listed below at home or school, and
2. play with equipment selected by teacher and parent(s).

Skills to Review

1. Level 1 kicking. Focus eyes on ball and
2. swinging lower leg forward, contact ball with foot and
3. kick ball so that it travels forward 8 feet.
4. Level 2 kicking. Step forward with nonkicking foot, eyes focused on rolling ball and
5. swing lower leg backward in preparation for the kick, and then
6. swing leg forward, contact ball with foot, and kick ball so that it travels forward 8 feet.

Action Words

Actions: Kick, move, step, stop, swing, walk

Objects: Ball, boxes, cones, foot, leg

Concepts: Backward, contact, forward, look, lower, ready, show me, sideways

Games

- Ball in the Basket
- Bowling Game
- Call Ball
- Circle Strike Ball
- Hot Potato
- Keep It Up
- Kick the Can
- Kick to the Target
- Modified Soccer
- Obstacle Course
- Scooter Kickball
- Stride Ball

TEACHING ACTIVITIES FOR MAINTENANCE

In Teaching

1. Provide the child with teaching cues (verbal and nonverbal, such as demonstration, modeling, imitating) for kicking a ball that involve the skill components the child has achieved in compatible teaching and play activities. Bring to the child's attention the skill components he or she has already achieved. Provide positive reinforcement and feedback for the child.

2. Use games that require kicking a ball and that involve imitating, modeling, and demonstrating.

3. Observe and assess each child's maintenance at the end of two weeks. Repeat at the end of four weeks (if maintained) and six weeks after initial date of attainment.

▲ Box in the skill level to be maintained on the child's Class Record of Progress. Note the date the child attained target level of performance (defined by teacher alone or co-planned with parents).

▲ Two weeks after attainment, observe the child. Is the level maintained? If child does not demonstrate the skill components at the desired level of performance, indicate the skill components that need reteaching or reinforcing in the comments sheet on the Class Record of Progress. Reschedule teaching time, and co-plan with parents the home activities necessary to reinforce child's achievement of the skill components and maintenance of attainment.

▲ Continue to observe the child, and reteach and reinforce until the child maintains that level of performance for six weeks.

▲ Plan teaching activities incorporating these components so that the child can continually use and reinforce them and can acquire new ones over the year.

▲ When the child can understand it, make a check-list poster illustrating the child's achievements. Bring the child's attention to these skill components in various compatible play and game activities throughout the year. Have the child help others—a partner or a small group.

In Co-Planning with Parent(s)

1. Encourage the parent(s) to reinforce the child's achievement of the skill components in everyday play and living activities in the home.

▲ Provide key action words for the parent(s) to emphasize.

▲ Give the parent(s) a list of play and games to use in playing with the child, thus reinforcing the skill components the child has achieved and needs support to maintain.

▲ Give the parent(s) a list of ball-kicking activities that can be done at home with the child, such as
   a. Kicking the nerf ball while holding it.
   b. Kicking the leaves on the ground.
   c. Kicking the ball up and down the hills.
   d. Kicking the ball to the four corners of the backyard.
   e. Kicking the ball across the street.

2. Set up a time every two weeks to interact with the parent(s) and exchange feedback on the child's progress.

HITTING A BALL: SKILL LEVEL 1

Performance Objective

The child with ability to grasp an object with both hands and move it forward can hit a stationary 2- to 4-inch ball with a hockey stick three consecutive times, demonstrating the following skill components:

Within a clear space of 15 feet, the child can

1. focus eyes on ball and,
2. holding the stick with both hands, move (swing, lift, push) it toward ball and
3. contact ball with blade of stick so that ball travels forward 6 feet.

Action Words

Actions: Hit, lift, move, push, swing

Objects: Ball, blade, edge

Concepts: Both, down, forward, look, one, ready, show me, through, under

Games

- Bat Ball
- Boundary Ball
- Call Ball
- Circle Strike Ball
- Floor Hockey
- Follow the String Golf
- Modified Tetherball
- Obstacle Course
- Putt It
- Red, Yellow, and Blue Cities
- Stride Ball
- Suspended Ball

TEACHING ACTIVITIES

If a child requires assistance to respond,

1. give verbal cues and physical assistance.
Manipulate or guide the child through the entire skill. Hold the child's wrists and hands with the hockey stick between them. Tell the child to focus eyes on the ball. Move the child's hands and stick backward and then forward to contact the ball with the blade of the stick. Give the child specific verbal instructions throughout (in sign language, bliss symbols, action cues), such as "Hit the ball with the stick," "Ready, go."

2. give verbal cues with demonstration.
Use a model or have the child watch you hit the ball with the hockey stick. Focus eyes on the ball, move hands with stick backward and then forward to contact the ball with the blade of the stick so that the ball travels forward 6 feet. Then have the child perform the action. Use specific verbal instructions (as in 1 above with the modeling).

If a child can respond without assistance,

3. give a verbal challenge in the form of a problem: "Who can . . . ?" "Show me how you can . . ."
a. Hit beanbags (pucks, paper balls) with the hockey stick.
b. Hit a large ball against the wall with the hockey stick. Retrieve the ball and hit it again.
c. Hit the balls that are placed on the beanbag. Retrieve the balls and hit them again.
d. Go and hit the balloons scattered around the room with the hockey stick.
e. With the stick, hit the ball off the table, under the chair, and around the cones.
f. Hit the ball with the stick around the diamond bases.
g. Variation: Hit the ball with the hockey stick to music.

4. introduce self-initiated learning activities.
Set up the equipment and space for hitting skills. Provide time at the beginning of the lesson and free time for independent learning after the child understands the skills to be used. You may ask the child to create a game activity to play alone or with others (partner or small group), using the equipment.

5. Variations: Set up an obstacle course that includes foam shapes and other play equipment. Play a game, such as Floor Hockey or Bat Ball, that incorporates hitting a ball.

HITTING A BALL: SKILL LEVEL 2

Performance Objective

The child with acquisition of Skill Level 1 can hit a directly rolled 2- to 4-inch ball with a hockey stick three consecutive times, demonstrating the following skill components:

Within a clear space of 15 feet, the child can

4. focus eyes on the ball and,

5. holding the stick with both hands, move stick backward in preparation to hit the ball and then

6. move the stick forward, contacting the ball with the blade of the stick so that the ball travels forward 15 feet.

Skills to Review

1. Focus eyes on ball and,

2. holding stick with both hands, move (swing, lift, push) stick toward ball and

3. contact ball with blade of stick so that ball travels forward 6 feet.

Action Words

Actions: Hit, lift, move, push, swing

Objects: Ball, blade, edge

Concepts: Both, down, forward, look, one, ready, show me, through, under

Games

● Bat Ball

● Boundary Ball

● Call Ball

● Circle Strike Ball

● Floor Hockey

● Follow the String Golf

● Hit Dodgeball

● Modified Tetherball

● Obstacle Course

● Putt It

● Red, Yellow, and Blue Cities

● Stride Ball

● Suspended Ball

TEACHING ACTIVITIES

If a child requires assistance to respond,

1. give verbal cues and physical assistance.
Manipulate or guide the child through the entire skill. Hold the child's wrists and hands with the hockey stick between them. Tell the child to focus eyes on the ball. Move the child's hands and stick backward and then forward to contact the ball with the blade of the stick. Give the child specific verbal instructions throughout (in sign language, bliss symbols, action cues), such as "Hit the ball with the stick," "Ready, go."

2. give verbal cues with demonstration.
Use a model or have the child watch you hit the ball with the hockey stick. Focus eyes on the ball, move hands with the stick backward and then forward to contact the ball with the blade of the stick so the ball travels forward 6 feet. Then have the child perform the action. Use specific verbal instructions (as in 1 above with the modeling).

If a child can respond without assistance,

3. give a verbal challenge in the form of a problem: "Who can . . . ?" "Show me how you can . . ."

a. Hit the rolling ball with the hockey stick to me.

b. Hit the rolling ball against the wall. Hit it again as it rolls back to you.

c. Stand on this line and, on the word *go,* hit your ball across the line to the goal.

d. Hit the rolling ball to the beat of the drum.

4. introduce self-initiated learning activities.
Set up the equipment and space for hitting skills.
Provide time at the beginning of the lesson and free time for independent learning after the child understands the skills to be used. You may ask the child to create a game activity to play alone or with others (partner or small group), using the equipment.

5. Variations: Set up an obstacle course that includes foam shapes and other play equipment. Play a game, such as Floor Hockey or Bat Ball that incorporates hitting a ball.

HITTING A BALL: SKILL LEVEL 3

Performance Objective

The child with acquisition of Skill Level 2 or a level of performance appropriate for the child's level of functioning can maintain that level over six weeks.

Given activities that require the skill, the child can

1. play two or more games listed below at home or school, and
2. play with equipment selected by teacher and parent(s).

Skills to Review

1. Level 1 hitting. Focus eyes on ball and,
2. holding stick with both hands, move (swing, lift, push) stick toward ball and
3. contact ball with blade of stick so that ball travels forward 6 feet.
4. Level 2 hitting. Focus eyes on ball and
5. holding stick with both hands, move stick backward in preparation to hit the ball and then
6. move stick forward, contacting ball with blade of stick so that ball travels forward 15 feet.

Action Words

Actions: Hit, lift, move, push, swing

Objects: Ball, blade, edge

Concepts: Both down, forward, look, one, ready, show me, through, under

Games

- Bat Ball
- Boundary Ball
- Call Ball
- Circle Strike Ball
- Floor Hockey
- Follow the String Golf
- Hit Dodgeball
- Modified Tetherball
- Obstacle Course
- Putt It
- Red, Yellow, and Blue Cities
- Stride Ball
- Suspended Ball

TEACHING ACTIVITIES FOR MAINTENANCE

In Teaching

1. Provide the child with teaching cues (verbal and nonverbal, such as demonstration, modeling, imitating) for hitting a ball that involve the skill components the child has achieved in compatible teaching and play activities. Bring to the child's attention the skill components he or she has already achieved. Provide positive reinforcement and feedback for the child.

2. Use games that require hitting a ball and that involve imitating, modeling, and demonstrating.

3. Observe and assess each child's maintenance at the end of two weeks. Repeat at the end of four weeks (if maintained) and six weeks after initial date of attainment.

▲ Box in the skill level to be maintained on the child's Class Record of Progress. Note the date the child attained target level of performance (defined by teacher alone or co-planned with parents).

▲ Two weeks after attainment, observe the child. Is the level maintained? If child does not demonstrate the skill components at the desired level of performance, indicate the skill components that need reteaching or reinforcing in the comments sheet on the Class Record of Progress. Reschedule teaching time, and co-plan with parents the home activities necessary to reinforce child's achievement of the skill components and maintenance of attainment.

▲ Continue to observe the child, and reteach and reinforce until the child maintains that level of performance for six weeks.

▲ Plan teaching activities incorporating these components so that the child can continually use and reinforce them and can acquire new ones over the year.

▲ When the child can understand it, make a checklist poster illustrating the child's achievements. Bring the child's attention to these skill components in various compatible play and game activities throughout the year. Have the child help others—a partner or a small group.

In Co-Planning with Parent(s)

1. Encourage the parent(s) to reinforce the child's achievement of the skill components in everyday play and living activities in the home.
▲ Provide key action words for the parent(s) to emphasize.
▲ Give the parent(s) a list of play and games to use in playing with the child, thus reinforcing the skill components the child has achieved and needs support to maintain.
▲ Give the parent(s) a list of ball-hitting activities that can be done at home with the child, such as
   a. Hitting the rolling ball with the hockey stick around the playground in the park.
   b. Hitting the rolling ball with the hockey stick up and down hills.
   c. Hitting the rolling ball with the hockey stick on the ice skating rink.
   d. Hitting the rolling ball with the hockey stick around the sprinklers in the yard.
   e. Hitting the rolling ball, catching it, and hitting it again.
   f. Playing a mock hockey game in the backyard with a sister or brother.
   g. Variation: Hitting the rolling ball to the beat of the drum.
2. Set up a time every two weeks to interact with the parent(s) and exchange feedback on the child's progress.

Checklists:
Individual and Class Records of Progress

A checklist is an objective score sheet for each ball-handling skill taught in the program. By observing and assessing each child's level of performance, you can identify the activities that will assist the child in reaching the performance objective. Use the same checklist to monitor the child's progress during instruction. When the child's performance level changes, you can upgrade the learning tasks (skill components) to the child's skill level.

To Begin

Decide on one or more ball-handling skills to be taught in the program. Become familiar with the description of the performance objective for each activity selected. Review the scoring key on the checklist. Plan assessing activities for the selected skills. The number will depend on the class size, the needs of the children, and the help available to you. Set up testing stations similar to the learning stations. Some teachers use free-play time (after setting up equipment for the objective to be tested) to observe the children.

1. Begin assessing at Skill Level 2 for the particular objective. If the child cannot perform at Skill Level 2 assess for Skill Level 1. If the child demonstrates the skill components for Skill Level 2 (i.e., with modeling, verbal cues, or no cues), the child has achieved functional competence. At the next skill level, Skill Level 3, the child demonstrates maintenance retention of the skill over time.

2. For some children with special needs, you may need to assess their levels of functioning before planning teaching activities. As in step 1, observe and assess the amount and type of assistance (cues) the child needs in descending order (i.e., from verbal cues to total manipulation).

Code	Amount and Type of Assistance
SI	Child initiates demonstrating the skill in the teaching and playing of activities
C	Child demonstrates the skill when given verbal cues with or without demonstration
A	Child demonstrates the skill when given partial assistance or total manipulation throughout the execution of the skill

Record, using the code above, the child's initial assistance level and progress in the comments column of the Class Record of Progress. For some children, this may be the most significant initial progress noted (i.e., from assistance to verbal cues and demonstration).

To Assess

1. Be sure all children are working on objectives at other stations while you are assessing at one station.

2. Make sure enough equipment is available for the skill to be tested.

3. For rolling, catching, kicking, and hitting a ball, have a small group of 3–4 children at a learning (testing) station. All other children in the class should be working at other learning stations. Mark a starting line, and have a teacher or aide stand or sit 10 or 15 feet away to receive ball (or place a target at that distance). Each child takes a turn on the command "go." At the end of the trials, record the child's performance on the score sheet.

4. For bouncing, line up a small group of 3–4 children at a learning (testing) station. Each child has a turn bouncing the ball for the designated trials. At the end of the trials, record each child's performance on the score sheet.

5. You may need to modify the assessing activity by using a larger or softer (nerf) ball, taking a child through the pattern or modeling the activity, or using sign language or an interpreter. Other modifications are an individual structured assessment with no distractions from other children or activities or free play with the equipment. Use mats or movable walls to help cut down on distractions.

To Adapt the Checklists

You can note children's skill components adaptations (i.e., physical devices or other changes) in the comments column on the Class Record of Progress. Other changes can be written under recommendations for individual children or the class. Modifications made for a child can be noted on the Individual Record of Progress. The Class Record of Progress can be adapted for an individual child. Record the name of the child rather than the class, and in the name column, record assessment dates. This adaptation may be needed for children whose progress is erratic, because it provides a base line assessment to find out where to begin teaching and evaluating the child's progress.

The Individual Record of Progress for the end-of-the-year report can be attached to the child's IEP (Individual Education Program) report. The record can also serve as a cumulative record for each child. Such records are very useful for new teachers, substitute teachers, aides, and volunteers, as well as parents. The format of the Individual Record of Progress can also be adapted for a Unit Report. The names of all the objectives for a unit—for example, walk-run endurance, running, catching a ball, and rolling a ball—are written rather than the names of the children. Book 8 illustrates the adaptation of the Individual Record of Progress for use in the Home Activities Program and for a Unit Report.

The checklists may be reproduced as needed to implement the play and motor skills program.

Class Record of Progress Report

CLASS: _____ DATE: _____

AGE/GRADE: _____ TEACHER: _____

SCHOOL: _____

OBJECTIVE: ROLLING A BALL

SCORING:

ASSESSMENT:

_____ Date

X = Achieved

O = Not Achieved

/ = Partially Achieved

REASSESSMENT:

_____ Date

⊗ = Achieved

Ø = Not Achieved

PRIMARY RESPONSES:

N = Not Attending

NR = No Response

UR = Unrelated Response

O = Other (Specify in comments)

Name	Graps ball with one or both hands and releases in forward direction. (1)	Rolls or pushes ball so that it travels an arm's length or more. (2)	Focuses eyes on the target. (3)	Rolls or pushes ball so that it travels 5 feet to a target. (4)	Rolls or pushes ball so that it travels 10 feet to a target. (5)	Two or more play or game activities at home or school demonstrating skill components over six-week period. (6)	Comments
	SKILL LEVEL 1		SKILL LEVEL 2 (Three Consecutive Times)			SKILL LEVEL 3	
1.							
2.							
3.							
4.							
5.							
6.							
7.							
8.							
9.							
10.							

Recommendations: Specific changes or conditions in planning for instructions, performance, or diagnostic testing procedures or standards. Please describe what worked best.

_____

_____

_____

_____

_____

CLASS RECORD OF PROGRESS REPORT

CLASS: _____   DATE: _____

AGE/GRADE: _____   TEACHER: _____

SCHOOL: _____

OBJECTIVE: THROWING A BALL

SCORING:	SKILL LEVEL 1			SKILL LEVEL 2				SKILL LEVEL 3	PRIMARY RESPONSES:
ASSESSMENT: _____ Date	Three Consecutive Times								N = Not Attending
X = Achieved									NR = No Response
O = Not Achieved									UR = Unrelated Response
/ = Partially Achieved									O = Other (Specify in comments)
REASSESSMENT: _____ Date	Grasping ball with one hand, releases ball in forward direction.	Arm extended forward as ball is released.	Ball travels forward 5 feet in air.	Focuses eyes on target.	Draws back arm in preparation to throw.	Shifts weight to nonthrowing side as ball is released.	Ball travels 10 feet in air toward target.	Two or more play or game activities at home or school demonstrating skill components over six-week period.	
NAME	1	2	3	4	5	6	7	8	COMMENTS
1.									
2.									
3.									
4.									
5.									
6.									
7.									
8.									
9.									
10.									

Scoring legend (reassessment): ⊗ = Achieved, Ø = Not Achieved

Recommendations: Specific changes or conditions in planning for instructions, performance, or diagnostic testing procedures or standards. Please describe what worked best.

_____

_____

_____

_____

_____

CLASS RECORD OF PROGRESS REPORT

CLASS: _____   DATE: _____

AGE/GRADE: _____   TEACHER: _____

SCHOOL: _____

OBJECTIVE: CATCHING A BALL

SCORING:	SKILL LEVEL 1		SKILL LEVEL 2				SKILL LEVEL 3	PRIMARY RESPONSES:
ASSESSMENT: _____ Date **X** = Achieved **O** = Not Achieved / = Partially Achieved REASSESSMENT: _____ Date ⊗ = Achieved Ø = Not Achieved	Three Consecutive Times							N = Not Attending NR = No Response UR = Unrelated Response O = Other (Specify in comments)
	Focuses eyes on ball.	Stops ball with hands or hands and arms.	Focuses eyes on ball.	Extends arms in preparation to catch ball, with elbows at sides.	Contacts and controls ball with hands or hands and arms after one bounce.	Bends elbows to absorb force of ball.	Two or more play or game activities at home or school demonstrating skill components over six-week period.	
NAME	1	2	3	4	5	6	7	COMMENTS
1.								
2.								
3.								
4.								
5.								
6.								
7.								
8.								
9.								
10.								

Recommendations: Specific changes or conditions in planning for instructions, performance, or diagnostic testing procedures or standards. Please describe what worked best.

_____

_____

_____

_____

_____

CLASS RECORD OF PROGRESS REPORT

CLASS: _____   DATE: _____

AGE/GRADE: _____   TEACHER: _____

SCHOOL: _____

OBJECTIVE: BOUNCING A BALL

SCORING: ASSESSMENT: _____ Date **X** = Achieved **O** = Not Achieved / = Partially Achieved REASSESSMENT: _____ Date ⊗ = Achieved Ø = Not Achieved	SKILL LEVEL 1		SKILL LEVEL 2		SKILL LEVEL 3	PRIMARY RESPONSES: N = Not Attending NR = No Response UR = Unrelated Response O = Other (Specify in comments)
	Three Consecutive Times					
	Focuses eyes on ball.	Hits or pushes ball downward with one or both hands three times.	Drops ball and hits or pushes it three or more times with eyes focused on ball.	Hits or pushes ball downward, hits ball three or more times as it bounces, with eyes focused on ball.	Two or more play or game activities at home or school demonstrating skill components over six-week period.	
NAME	1	2	3	4	5	COMMENTS
1.						
2.						
3.						
4.						
5.						
6.						
7.						
8.						
9.						
10.						

Recommendations: Specific changes or conditions in planning for instructions, performance, or diagnostic testing procedures or standards. Please describe what worked best.

_____

_____

_____

_____

_____

CLASS RECORD OF PROGRESS REPORT

CLASS: _____ DATE: _____

AGE/GRADE: _____ TEACHER: _____

SCHOOL: _____

OBJECTIVE: KICKING A BALL

SCORING:	SKILL LEVEL 1			SKILL LEVEL 2			SKILL LEVEL 3	PRIMARY RESPONSES:
ASSESSMENT: _____ Date	Three Consecutive Times							N = Not Attending
X = Achieved								NR = No Response
O = Not Achieved								UR = Unrelated Response
/ = Partially Achieved								O = Other (Specify in comments)
REASSESSMENT: _____ Date	Focuses eyes on ball.	Swings lower leg forward to contact ball with foot.	Kicks ball so that it travels forward 8 feet.	Steps forward with nonkicking foot, eyes focused on rolling ball.	Swings lower leg backward in preparation for the kick.	Swings leg forward, contacts ball with foot, kicks ball so that it travels forward 8 feet.	Two or more play or game activities at home or school demonstrating skill components over six-week period.	
NAME	1	2	3	4	5	6	7	COMMENTS
1.								
2.								
3.								
4.								
5.								
6.								
7.								
8.								
9.								
10.								

Recommendations: Specific changes or conditions in planning for instructions, performance, or diagnostic testing procedures or standards. Please describe what worked best.

_____

_____

_____

_____

_____

CLASS RECORD OF PROGRESS REPORT

CLASS: _____   DATE: _____

AGE/GRADE: _____   TEACHER: _____

SCHOOL: _____

OBJECTIVE: HITTING A BALL

SCORING: ASSESSMENT: _____ Date **X** = Achieved **O** = Not Achieved **/** = Partially Achieved REASSESSMENT: _____ Date ⊗ = Achieved Ø = Not Achieved	SKILL LEVEL 1			SKILL LEVEL 2			SKILL LEVEL 3	PRIMARY RESPONSES: N = Not Attending NR = No Response UR = Unrelated Response O = Other (Specify in comments)
	Three Consecutive Times							
	Focuses eyes on ball.	Holding stick with both hands, moves (swings, lifts, pushes) stick toward ball.	Contacts ball with blade of stick so that ball travels forward 6 feet.	Focuses eyes on ball.	Holding stick with both hands, moves stick backward in preparation to hit the ball.	Moves stick forward, contacting ball with blade of stick so that ball travels forward 15 feet.	Two or more play or game activities at home or school demonstrating skill components over six-week period.	
NAME	1	2	3	4	5	6	7	COMMENTS
1.								
2.								
3.								
4.								
5.								
6.								
7.								
8.								
9.								
10.								

Recommendations: Specific changes or conditions in planning for instructions, performance, or diagnostic testing procedures or standards. Please describe what worked best.

_____

_____

_____

_____

_____

INDIVIDUAL RECORD OF PROGRESS

Area: Ball-Handling Skills

CHILD: _____

LEVEL: _____

YEAR: _____

TEACHER: _____

SCHOOL: _____

Marking Period	Date
Fall Conference (white)	from ____ to ____
Winter Conference (yellow)	from ____ to ____
Spring Conference (pink)	from ____ to ____
End-of-Year (cumulative) Report (blue)	from ____ to ____

Preprimary Play and Motor Skills Activity Program

The Individual Record of Progress lists all of the objectives in which your child receives instruction during the play and motor skills program. The information reported on your child's Individual Record of Progress shows your child's entry performance and progress for a marking period. The end-of-the-year report represents your child's Individual Education Program (IEP) for the objectives selected and taught during the year.

Each objective is broken into small, measurable steps or skill components. This assists the teacher to assess what your child already knew before teaching began and to determine which step to start teaching first. One of the following symbols is marked by each step or skill component of the objective:

X = The child already knew how to perform this step before teaching it began.

O = The child did not know how to perform this step before teaching it began or after instruction of it ended.

⊗ = The child did not know how to perform this step before teaching it began, but did learn how to do it during the instruction period.

This information should be helpful to you in planning home activities to strengthen your child's play and motor skills.

Comments

_____

_____

_____

_____

_____

_____

_____

_____

ROLLING A BALL

Date: _____

Within a space of 10 feet,
Three consecutive times

____ Grasps ball with one or both hands and releases in forward direction.

____ Rolls or pushes ball so that it travels an arm's length or more.

____ Focuses eyes on target.

____ Rolls or pushes ball so that it travels 5 feet to a target.

____ Rolls or pushes ball so that it travels 10 feet to a target.

____ Demonstrates above skills in two or more play or game activities at home or school over a six-week period.

THROWING A BALL

Date: _____

Within a space of 20 feet,
Three consecutive times

____ While grasping ball with one hand, releases ball in forward direction.

____ Arm extended forward as ball is released.

____ Ball travels forward 5 feet in air.

____ Focuses eyes on target.

____ Draws back arm in preparation to throw.

____ Shifts weight to nonthrowing side as ball is released.

____ Ball travels 10 feet in air toward target.

____ Demonstrates above skills in two or more play or game activities at home or school over a six-week period.

CATCHING A BALL

Date: _____

Within a space of 15 feet,
Three consecutive times

Rolled Ball

____ Focuses eyes on ball.

____ Stops ball with hands or hands and arms.

Bounced Ball

____ Focuses eyes on ball.

____ Extends arms in preparation to catch ball, elbows at sides.

____ Contacts and controls ball with hands or hands and arms after one bounce.

____ Bends elbows to absorb force of ball.

____ Demonstrates above skills in two or more play or game activities at home or school over a six-week period.

BOUNCING A BALL

Date: _____

*Within a space of 15 feet,
Three consecutive times*

____ Focuses eyes on ball.

____ Hits or pushes downward
with one or both hands
three times.

____ Drops ball and hits or
pushes ball three or more
times, with *eyes focused
on ball.*

____ Hits or pushes ball downward, hits ball three or more
times as it bounces, with
eyes focused on ball.

____ Demonstrates above skills in
two or more play or game
activities at home or school
over a six-week period.

KICKING A BALL

Date: _____

*Within a space of 15 feet,
Three consecutive times*

____ Focuses eyes on ball.

____ Swings lower leg forward to
contact ball with foot.

____ Kicks ball so that it travels
forward eight feet.

____ Steps forward with nonkicking foot, eyes focused on
rolling ball.

____ Swings lower leg backward
in preparation for the kick.

____ Swings leg forward, contacts
ball with foot, kicks ball so
that it travels forward 8 feet.

____ Demonstrates above skill in
two or more play or game
activities at home or school
over a six-week period.

HITTING A BALL

Date: _____

*Within a space of 15 feet,
Three consecutive times*

____ Focuses eyes on ball.

____ Holding stick with both
hands, moves (swings, lifts,
pushes) stick toward ball.

____ Contacts ball with blade of
stick so that ball travels forward 6 feet.

____ Focuses eyes on ball.

____ Holding stick with both
hands, moves stick back-
ward in preparation to hit
the ball.

____ Moves stick forward, contacting ball with blade of
stick so that ball travels
forward 15 feet.

____ Demonstrates above skill in
two or more play or game
activities at home or school
over a six-week period.

Games

Game Selection

The following game sheets will help you select and plan game activities. They include the names of the games in alphabetical order, formation, directions, equipment, ball-handling skills, and type of play activity. Consider the following points when selecting games:

1. Skills and objectives of your program

2. Interest of the child

3. Equipment and rules

4. Adaptability of physical difficulty level in order to match each child's ability

5. Activity for healthy growth and development

6. Social play skill development, such as taking turns, sharing equipment, playing with others, and following and leading

Games can foster creativity. Children enjoy making up, interpreting, and creating their own activities, whether playing alone, with a partner, or with a small group. The time you take to provide opportunities for each child to explore and create will be well spent. One further note. Children can easily create or adapt games matched to their mobility, even if limited by crutches, braces, or wheelchairs. Ball-handling activities involve moving from here to there. These children easily comprehend how to get to "there" with their own expertise for movement.

Following are some suggestions for adapting the physical difficulty level of games and a sequential list of social play development:

Adapting Games

To Change	Use	Example
1. Boundaries	Larger or smaller space	For target practice, line up children 5 feet, then 10 feet, from target.
2. Equipment	Larger or smaller sizes, weights, or heights, or specially adapted equipment for some children (such as guiderails, inclines rather than stairs, brightly colored mats)	Use different sizes of balls in Net Ball or Shotgun game.
3. Rules	More or fewer rules	In Stride Ball, partners pass ball first two times, then four times.

To Change	Use	Example
4. Actions	More or fewer actions to be performed at one time; play in stationary positions, using various body parts	In Cage Ball game, push cage ball with one hand, then two hands.
5. Time of play	Longer or shorter time; frequent rest periods	In Call Ball game, toss ball to children for 10 minutes, then for 15 minutes.

To adapt games to other special needs, you might also use buddies and spotters, sign language gestures, or place the child near leader.

Sequential Development of Social Play

Sequence	Description	Example of Play Activity
Individual Play	Child plays alone and independently with toys that are different from those used by other children within speaking distance.	Child plays with beanbags in classroom, while other children play with different balls.
Parallel Play	Child plays independently beside, rather than with, other children.	Child plays with beanbags alongside other children who are also playing with beanbags. No interaction between children.
Associate Play	Child plays with other children. There is interaction between children, but there are no common goals.	Child plays and follows other children bouncing or kicking balls.
Cooperative Play	Child plays within a group organized for playing formal games. Group is goal directed.	Children play Kick the Can or Keep It Up with one or two leaders.

Game Sheet Lesson Plans

Games	Organization	Description/Instructions	Equipment	Skills	Type of Play Activity
Ball in the Basket	Line T × × × × × → ⊙ 1 2 3 4 5	Children stand behind each other in line. Last child rolls ball to child nearest target. That child rolls ball to hit target. Teacher returns ball and game starts again.	Ball, target (box, basket)	Roll ball, throw ball, kick ball, catch ball	Relay; partner, small group, large group
Ball Pass Relay	Line start × → × → × end	Organize children into a line. Tell them, "Turn around and roll ball to student behind you. Get ready, set, go. Stop when last person in line has ball."	4"– 6" balls	Roll ball, throw ball	Relay; small group, large group
Bat Ball	Scatter with partner × | × × | × × | ×	Divide groups into pairs, each with a ball. Put a strip of tape on floor between them. Have players hit the ball back and forth to each other's "court," using open hand or paddles.	7" rubber ball for each pair; paddles	Hit ball	Partners, small group, large group
Beach Ball Push	Lines × × × ————— × × ×	Seat children in two rows with legs apart. Toss ball over center line, and have children use arms to push ball over line to other side.	Inflated balloons or beach balls	Roll ball	Partners, small group, large group

Game Sheet Lesson Plans

Games	Organization	Description/Instructions	Equipment	Skills	Type of Play Activity
Bounce Ball Relay	Lines 	Teacher says, "When I say 'go,' run to the circle, bounce the ball one time, and run back. Then give the ball to the next person."	8" balls; circles	Bounce ball, run	Relay; partners, small group, large group
Boundary Ball	Scatter 	Divide children into two teams. Say, "Take ball and throw it over the center line. Other team will try to catch the ball. Object of game is to keep the ball from touching the floor on your side."	6" play yard ball	Throw ball, bounce ball, catch ball	Small group, large group, team
Bowling Game	Line or circle 	Children stand behind line facing pins, or in circle around pins. Children roll ball at pins, trying to knock them down. Reset pins and return ball.	Balls; cones or pins	Roll ball, kick ball, hit ball, throw ball	Individual, partner, small group, large group
Cage Ball Roll/Push	Line 	Arrange children in line. Have each child roll or push cage ball with both hands around the other children and then go back to start.	Cage ball	Roll/push ball	Individual, partner, small group, large group

Game Sheet Lesson Plans

Games	Organization	Description/Instructions	Equipment	Skills	Type of Play Activity
Call Ball	Circle 	Join hands and form circle. Drop hands. Leader calls name of a child and tosses ball to him or her. Child tries to catch ball and toss it back to leader. Leader then tosses ball to next child.	Ball, beanbag	Throw ball, catch ball, kick ball	Partner, small group, large group
Catching Balloons and Soap Bubbles	Lines or scatter 	Blow soap bubbles for children to chase and catch in their hands. Let children blow bubbles for partners to chase and catch. Blow up balloons and toss them into air for children to chase and catch.	Balloons, bubbles	Catch ball	Individual, partner, small group, large group
Circle Strike Ball	Circle 	Join hands to make circle. Release them and sit down. Push ball into circle, and have each child roll ball across the circle.	Ball	Roll ball, kick ball, hit ball, bounce ball	Partner, small group, large group
Cleaning out the Backyard	Scatter 	Divide class into two teams on each side of net. Scatter balls and say, "Look at all these balls messing up our yard. Throw them all out. When I blow the whistle, throw as many as you can across the net. When I blow the whistle again, stop."	2 (or more) 4"–6" balls; volleyball net across room 3'–4' above floor	Throw ball	Partner, small group, large group

GAME SHEET LESSON PLANS

GAMES	ORGANIZATION	DESCRIPTION/INSTRUCTIONS	EQUIPMENT	SKILLS	TYPE OF PLAY ACTIVITY
Diamond Relay	Scatter	First person up kicks the ball out into field, runs to first base, second, third, and home. Can award "home run" for each runner who makes it home before ball is returned.	4 bases, 8" ball	Kick ball, roll ball	Small group; large group
Floor Hockey (modification of field hockey)	Scatter	Put puck into goal. Encourage children to hit puck toward cardboard box lying on side. Can use goalkeeper to hit puck away as it gets near.	Hockey sticks; soft ball or hockey puck; large cardboard box	Hit ball	Small group, large group
Follow the String Golf	Line	Zigzag a rope around room. Instruct children to hit at ball while following the zigzag path.	Small ball or newspaper balls; rope; stick or golf club	Hit ball	Individual, partner, small group, large group
Hot Potato	Circle	Join hands to make a circle. Release hands. Roll ball around circle very quickly. Tell children it is a hot potato. Can use music: child with ball when music stops is out for one turn. Can use two balls.	Ball	Roll ball, throw ball, kick ball, catch ball, bounce ball	Partner, small group, large group

GAME SHEET LESSON PLANS

GAMES	ORGANIZATION	DESCRIPTION/INSTRUCTIONS	EQUIPMENT	SKILLS	TYPE OF PLAY ACTIVITY
Keep It Up	Line (□ ← X, □ ← X, □ X, □ X; 5–10 ft.)	Tell children, "When I say 'go,' hit the ball at the target as many times as you can before I say 'stop.' If ball rolls away, get it."	4 bases; 8" ball	Kick ball, roll ball	Small group, large group
Kick the Can	Line (X X X → ⊠)	Arrange children in a line. Encourage children to kick can toward a goal. Tell them to chase can as it rolls and kick it again.	Coffee cans or juice cans	Kick ball, run	Relay; partner, small group, large group
Kick to the Target	Lines (target ← 10–30 ft.; X X X rows)	Tell children, "Kick the ball at the target. Every time you hit it, you get a point. How many points can you get?"	Balls, taped target	Kick ball	Relay; individual, partner, small group, large group
Leader, Class	Lines (XXXX ← X leader, XXXX ← X leader)	Divide class into equal teams. Line teammates behind one another. One child on each team is leader and stands 5 feet from first person on team. Leader throws ball to first team member, who throws ball to next team member and sits down. Throw and catch until whole team is sitting.	3"– 4" ball	Throw ball, catch ball	Relay; small group, large group

GAME SHEET LESSON PLANS

GAMES	ORGANIZATION	DESCRIPTION/INSTRUCTIONS	EQUIPMENT	SKILLS	TYPE OF PLAY ACTIVITY
Modified Soccer	Scattered	Children kick ball with various parts of foot and run after ball, kicking it toward goal.	Soccer ball	Kick ball, run	Individual, small group, large group
Modified Tetherball	Circle	Children stand in circle around tetherball stand. Encourage them to hit ball as it swings around, using their hands.	Tetherball, stand	Hit ball	Small group, large group
Monkey in the Middle	Circle	Children begin in circle with one child in center. Have children throw ball over child in center. Center child tries to catch ball. If successful, that child changes places with child who threw ball.	Newspaper balls	Catch ball	Small group, large group
Net Ball	Scatter	Divide children into two teams. Say, "When this team has ball, they throw it over the net, and the other team tries to catch ball before it hits the floor or after bouncing only once. If they let ball hit the floor, then other team gets point."	3"–4" ball, volleyball net across room at 10' height	Throw ball over net	Small group, large group

GAME SHEET LESSON PLANS

GAMES	ORGANIZATION	DESCRIPTION/INSTRUCTIONS	EQUIPMENT	SKILLS	TYPE OF PLAY ACTIVITY
Obstacle Course	(diagram: start, bench, hoop, cones, pins)	Children roll ball under bench into hoop, around cones, and hit the pins.	Benches, hoops, cones, pins	All ball-handling skills	Relay; individual, partner, small group, large group
Paper Ball Play	Line (diagram: 10–40 ft.)	Arrange line so that all children will throw at cans on chairs. Say, "Throw at the can and try to knock down." Increase distance from chair.	Cans or milk cartons, beanbags or paper balls or 3"–4" balls	Throw ball	Relay; small group, large group
Push Ball Relay	Line (diagram: goal)	Each child hits the ball over a goal line. Can put obstacles between starting line and goal.	8" ball; stick for each group; cones	Hit ball	Individual, partner, small group, large group
Putt It	Line (diagram: hole, tee)	Children form line behind tee. Sink coffee can into sand or tape boxes on floor. Each child has 3 pucks to hit into container.	Pucks; pushbroom; coffee can or box; construction paper taped to floor as putting tee	Hit ball	Small group, large group

Game Sheet Lesson Plans

Games	Organization	Description/Instructions	Equipment	Skills	Type of Play Activity
Red, Yellow, and Blue Cities	Scattered	Children stand 20–30 feet apart. Say, "We are going to pretend that Blue City (Child #1) is sending a letter (puck) to Red City (Child #2). Red City then sends puck to Yellow City (Child #3)." Each child sends and receives letter with hockey stick.	Hockey sticks; plastic pucks; colored cards	Hit ball	Partner, small group, large group
Scoop Catch	Lines or scatter	Divide class into pairs. Each child has a scoop and a ball. Have each child take turns throwing ball and catching it in scoop. Ask, "How many catches can you make?"	Plastic scoops (plastic milk bottles); tennis balls	Catch ball, throw ball	Partners, small group, large group
Scooter Kickball	Scatter	Children sit on scooterboards and kick toward goal.	Scooterboard for each child; ball; box lying on side (goal)	Kick ball	Individual, partners, small group, large group

GAME SHEET LESSON PLANS

GAMES	ORGANIZATION	DESCRIPTION/INSTRUCTIONS	EQUIPMENT	SKILLS	TYPE OF PLAY ACTIVITY
Shotgun	Lines	Have children stand around the outside of gym, facing wall. Say, "Throw ball at the wall as hard as you can. When you 'blast' the wall, get your ball and blast again. Now move back a step. Throw from there as hard as you can."	Paper balls, bean-bags, or 3"–4" balls	Throw ball, catch ball, bounce ball	Individual, partners, small group, large group
Stride Ball	Partners	Divide children into pairs facing each other, standing with legs apart. One child takes ball and rolls it between partner's legs. After ball passes through, partner retrieves ball and rolls it between first child's legs.	3"–4" balls	Roll ball, bounce ball, catch ball, hit ball, kick ball, throw ball	Relay; partners, small group, large group
Suspended Ball	Line	Hit ball with hand or fist; bat it with stick.	Suspended ball	Hit ball	Individual, partners, small group
Target Bowling	Lines	Divide class into teams according to ability. More skilled start at 50', others at 25'. Say, "When I say start, stand behind line and roll ball to target. If you hit target, you get 1 point. You get three turns. Then go to the end of the line."	1'–3' target, one 3"–4" or 8"–12" ball per team	Roll ball	Small group, large group

Game Sheet Lesson Plans

Games	Organization	Description/Instructions	Equipment	Skills	Type of Play Activity
Target Practice	Lines 8 ft. target 5 ft.	Children line up 5 feet from target. Throw ball at target and try to hit it. Children get a point every time they hit target.	3"–4" balls; masking tape; 8-square-ft. target placed 1 foot off floor	Throw ball for accuracy	Relay; individual, partners, small group, large group
Throw (kick), Rebound, Catch	Line	Children throw (or kick) the ball at the wall and then try to catch ball.	6" balls	Throw ball, catch ball, kick ball	Individual, partners, small group
Toss-Jump-Pick	Line beanbags	Children stand in line side by side. Each tosses beanbag (ball) in front of them on floor and tries to jump over it. If child touches beanbag or can't jump over it, then he or she picks beanbag up, throws it, and jumps again.	Beanbag, balls	Throw ball	Relay; individual, partners, small group, large group